MAJ - GENERAL W.H.C. RAMSDEN, C.B.E., D.S.O., M.C.

Published by

The Naval & Military Press Ltd

Unit 5 Riverside, Brambleside
Bellbrook Industrial Estate
Uckfield, East Sussex
TN22 1QQ England

Tel: +44 (0)1825 749494

www.naval-military-press.com
www.nmarchive.com

THE STORY OF "FIFTY DIV"

by AUBREY HAMMOND

(Allied Newspapers, Great Britain)

I.

Two superimposed letters T, which appear on small signposts stuck in the sand, strike a pleasant homely note for the wanderer along roads and tracks in the Western Desert, where everything else seems grim and forbidding. One T stands for Trent, the other for Tweed — the old boundaries of Northumbria. Although this suggestion of geographical area may not altogether be adequate to designate the 50th (Northumbrian) Division today since some of the men come from all parts of Britain, an observer from the North feels cheered by the mere sight of it.

Knowing that he is among friends with very much his own outlook — although inevitable losses and other circumstances of war have tended to alter the original constitution of the Division, North-countrymen are still in the majority — he is reminded of breezy moors and lovely dales, of green hills (in startling contrast to the arid escarpments he sees in the distance) and of a sea which, although it cannot attain the miraculous blue of the Mediterranean, seems better to fit the English temperament. Then, when he has bumped along a dusty track, he finds himself amongst stalwart men who talk to him in simple direct language of a hundred and one adventures; men who have already fought and beaten the Germans and Italians and will fight them to the end; men who from Gazala onwards have forced gaps in the enemy's lines and made bridgeheads round them; men who have remained firing until there were no more shells or bullets to fire, even though their positions at times were overrun. They have shivered in the desert's cold, grilled in its blistering heat. They are usually to be found in the forefront of the battle, wherever it is — the Gazala line, the "Cauldron," Mersa Matruh, El Alamein. No troops have a higher reputation for fighting qualities and outstanding achievement.

When I visit South African, Australian, Indian, and particularly New Zealand units, which include some of the finest soldiers in the desert, I am filled with admiration for the men and for their prowess in battle. But the 50th Division has a special niche in English minds and hearts and when I began to write this account of some of the experiences of the Green Howards, East Yorks, Durham Light Infantry and other attached units, I realised that it would be read by many thousands of people who have as deep a personal interest in the Division itself as in the men I was writing about. I am told that in many letters from home inquiring about the welfare of sons and husbands, there is often a paragraph or two referring with pride to the achievements, so far as they have become known, of "Fifty Div."

For those who may have no reason to identify themselves with the Division in this way, it needs emphasis that, despite the presence of so many Empire troops, men from the Homeland still predominate numerically over the forces of the United Nations in the desert field, though it is rather a noteworthy fact that the only United Kingdom Infantry Division fighting the enemy anywhere in the world for many difficult months was the 50th.

Most people now know the names of the regiments making up this Division but, unfortunately, there was a time when most people did not, and when I spent some time with the Green Howards in the Gazala line during the long period of relative lull, I could only refer to them in articles written then as "North Country" troops. Later the authorities wisely decided that names of units could be given in some instances and you may imagine the pleasure the men felt when, for the first time, they heard mention of their units over the wireless' "Now my wife will know I was in the Gazala line,'. said one officer. It's probably true she knew all the time for it's astonishing how two and two are put together at home, however scanty the information in letters and newspapers.

For another reason, Durham Light Infantrymen were delighted when it was announced : "Among the regiments are D.L.I., Coldstream Guards, Scots Guards, etc..." But, indeed, the D.L.I. like the other constituent units has earned a fine name for itself here where it is numbered among the elect. It was the only regiment in the army to be represented in France by as many as seven battalions, six of these being Territorial. And, incidentally, the majority of the many battalions of D.L.I., Green Howards and East Yorks in the Middle East are Territorial.

Reprinted now in pamphlet form, just as it was used in several newspapers at home for the readers for whom it was solely intended, this account may come into the hands of many who have been personally concerned with what has been described all too inadequately. That is a stern test indeed.

Were I now a soldier I should dislike and rightly condemn any highly coloured descriptive matter which we journalists call "Guff;" any attempt to gloss or slur over unpleasant facts; any forced cheerfulness not based on solid reality. I have tried to avoid such irritating pitfalls, but I realise only too well that the story is most incomplete. Still, the soldier reader will fill in the gaps from his own knowledge and memory, supply the deficiences and, better than that, build up — possibly on the basis of this record — his own story which he can tell and retell in the years to come.

Several names mentioned in connection with acts of gallantry and resource have been picked out from a great many examples almost at random, since it would not be possible to give complete citations which were all published at the time they were officially issued. But there is one name which will always be remembered with pride in his regiment, his division and in Newcastle-on-Tyne, his home town where he sold newspapers as a boy.

It is that of Private Adam Herbert Wakenshaw of the Durham Light Infantry who received the posthumous reward of the Victoria Cross. The strength of the tie binding the people of the North with the Division in the Desert has been strinkingly exemplified by the way in which Newcastle citizens took immediate steps to ensure the welfare of the hero's widow and of his two orphaned children.

How Wakenshaw won the V.C. is a story which is not only remarkable in itself but provides the supreme example of those qualities of courage and endurance which have been shown again and again in the Division during the desert campaign.

Although its place here should rightly be with the account of operations in the Mersa Matruh area, it is fitting accordingly that it should appear out of its context.

On June 27, 1942, Private Wakenshaw was a member of the crew of a two-pounder anti-tank gun, sited on a forward slope south of Mersa Matruh.

Shortly after dawn the enemy attacked bringing a tracked vehicle towing a light gun which was brought to within short range of our position. The anti-tank gun opened fire and succeeded in putting a round through the engine of the enemy vehicle.

Another enemy mobile gun then came into action and all the members of the two-pounder anti-tank gun crew, including Private Wakenshaw, were seriously wounded or killed and the gun silenced. The enemy then moved forward towards their damaged tractor in order to get the light gun into action against our infantry.

Realising the danger to his comrades, under intense mortar and artillery fire which swept the gun site, Private Wakenshaw crawled back to his gun. Although his left arm was blown off above the elbow he loaded the gun with one arm and fired five more rounds. These succeeded in setting the tractor on fire and damaged the light gun.

A near miss then killed the gun aimer and blew Private Wakenshaw away from the gun giving him further severe wounds. Undeterred he slowly dragged himself back to the gun, placed a round in the breach, and was preparing to fire when a direct hit on the ammunition killed him and destroyed the gun.

The body of Private Wakenshaw was later found stretched out on the back of the breach block beside the ammunition box.

This act of conspicuous gallantry and outstanding devotion to duty, on the part of Private Wakenshaw, prevented the enemy from bringing their light gun into action against our infantry which were only 200 yards away. Through his courage and self-sacrifice he saved the lives of many of his comrades.

2

The 50th Division came out to the Middle East early in 1941. In France its most notable achievement, perhaps, had been filling a gap south of Arras, for which purpose it had been rushed from Belgium. Its action here was only on a small scale, one of the few purely infantry attracks made by the British in France, and although it was not supported by tanks it was partially successful. The Division was dived-bombed, but as there were no troops available in support and the general situation was deteriorating, it was withdrawn to Vimy, where it fought a notable rearguard action. The 50th was one of the last two divisions to leave Dunkirk. Then there was a reorganisation from July, 1940, until the spring of the following year, when one brigade came straight out into the desert.

Cyprus was very much a danger point then and other brigades were sent there. The men spent their time making the island a fortress, and in their leisure hours enjoyed, on the whole, a pastoral life amid groves of vines and pomegranates.

In autumn last year while some of the Division was in Iraq, another part was concerned with General Ritchie's offensive in Libya, holding positions at Tengeda through which the British Forces later withdrew. Afterwards it laid part of the minefields forming the defences of Bir Hacheim, which were subsequently to attain fame. In February this year the Division was together and complete in the desert, 150 Brigade having rejoined it, and, as well as operating columns forward in no-man's-land with the South Africans and Fighting French as near neighbours to the north and south, it took over from 4th Indian Division a series of defensive localities in the central sector of the Gazala line.

Territorials from Hull, the East Riding and Durham were blooded in major desert warfare when they carried out in March a three column operation named "Full-size". A column from 150 Brigade raided Martuba aerodrome, another column from 151 Brigade attacked positions at Gabr Aleima and a third column from 69 Brigade cooperated with it. Considering the amount of dive-bombing, casualties at Martuba were not high. The aerodrome raids yielded prisoners and five 76 mm. guns.

During the following two months when there were no major operations I spent some time with the Green Howards and saw at close quarters the arduous column and patrol work that was going on. The Division was somewhat handicapped by ageing vehicles, although these displayed remarkable powers of resistance to wear and tear caused by constant column and patrol activity and they had already been through several campaigns, twice having made journeys to Iraq. "Fifty Div." had lost all its original vehicles in France and had handed over new ones to succeeding units in Cyprus.

I will not go into detail into the circumstances of the enemy's break-through in the central sector of the Gazala line. Much is known about it already and has been related : much remains obscure and cannot yet be told. But there is one interesting fact.

Apparently the Italian Trento and Sobrata divisions were entirely deceived about our strength on this front, principally because we had outposts, which had not been penetrated at any time, 400 to 500 yards in front of one brigade, of which the present divisional commander was then Brigadier. The enemy was, in fact, ignorant of the existence of a whole brigade.

The enemy attack was delivered in the late afternoon of May 27 on the whole Divisional front. It was held up on the front of 151 Brigade on the line of the outposts. On the 69 Brigade front we kept the enemy at a distance though no actual outposts were held. Elsewhere certain of our formations were overrun and had a bad time. Yet, though some units were isolated and encircled by the enemy who was in overwhelming numbers, it took many days to reduce them, for they fought on doggedly.

I sat on a sandy mound the other day with a colonel's batman who gave me his own story of what happened. Private Davison, of the Green

Howards, who comes from Middlesbrough, told me that on returning from a column patrol into no-man's-land his unit got the Tanks Alert warning. Later they learned that the enemy had made a 20-mile gap in the minefield on Trigh Capuzzo and was advancing from the direction of Rotunda Mteifel.

"We were attacked on the following morning," said Davison, "but repulsed two enemy attempts to get through. Just at that time General Cruewell, Rommel's right-hand man, was brought in by one of our carriers. His Fieseler-Storch aircraft had been hit by a burst from a German gun (there are other versions of this incident) and as I was near him I saw how furious he was.

"We had fine cooperation from the R.A.F. who did some marvellously accurate work considering the short distance between the forces. Eventually, after an artillery bombardment, the enemy poured in from all sides. Armoured cars and lorried infantry advanced, while Stukas dive-bombed. The enemy's method seemed to be to establish crossfire from the positions first taken on to further positions. We chaps were crouched in trenches for six days. Perhaps our biggest personal trouble was that we couldn't get any tea. For food we had battle rations. The Royal Tank Regiment unit we had with us had only one tank left after fierce fighting.

"The enemy infiltrated, took prisoners, and I and some others were put in the bag.' We were escorted to a wadi and taken on a circular route march, after which we were photographed. When we saw our own guns shelling the enemy's transport, I and two other chaps walked in the direction of the firing. We lay down in a minefield for a while and three or four enemy patrols passed without spotting us. Then we were joined by four R.T.R. men, three more Green Howards, a Cheshire chap and three gunners. I made a plan of escape which we all discussed as we lay doggo from dawn till dusk. After drawing water from a certain point, we crept along in groups of two but lay down again and waited till morning as the enemy's white flares were going up rather too freely. By this time we were tired, our feet were aching and we were short of water and food. We had already walked a good way but we took a chance and trudged on through five of our minefields in single file. The sight of one of our carriers cheered us considerably and we did the final mile or so with a spurt, arriving in the Brigade box' in grand spirits, dead right, as though we had been using a compass."

Davison added that one German officer whom he took to be a General came up to him and said in excellent English : "Damned good fight ; very clean and very sporting."

Between May 27 and June 2, the enemy made no progress on the front of 151 and 69 Brigades although two Italian divisions were brought up.

During this period a series of defended localities was constructed to the East of 69 Brigade position facing south and linking up 69 Brigade with Acroma, therby covering our communications with Tobruk.

The Division had many successes against the Pavia Division, capturing 250 prisoners in one attack and destroying a whole battalion in another. "In fact," the Divisional Commander told me, "up to June 14 we were on top of the world and scored big successes in attacks south, east and west, until it was decided we must fight our way out."

From the opening of the enemy's offensive until the date of the fighting withdrawal — some aspects of which I shall describe presently—belong almost countless deeds of courage under great difficulties and stress. Some of these deeds have been recorded, but there are many more which will probably never be known to the world.

There is the story of Private Harold Robinson, East Yorkshire Regiment, who was awarded the M.M. for saving the lives of many wounded. In one case, with only scissors and clasp knives, he amputated and tended the arm of one man who would certainly have died had he not received this prompt attention.

Later on I shall write something about the magnificent work done by the divisional R.A.S.C. in the desert generally, but here is an episode which rightly belongs to the Gazala period and the story is of how Major John Walter Rea, R.A.S.C., won the D.S.O.

On May 31 it was necessary for a maintenance convoy to get through to a brigade which had been surrounded and cut off. Under Major Rea, 40 lorries loaded with supplies set out and tried by every route to get through to the brigade, going through areas in which there were enemy armoured forces, but without success. After three days Major Rea left his convoy under the protection of forces near Bir Hacheim and set out to reconnoitre the route back. He was attacked by enemy armoured elements, but when he returned safely with his driver the convoy could not be found. Major Rea then came upon undamaged enemy tanks, three British ambulances and four British lorries which had previously been captured by the enemy. He disabled the tanks and immobilised all the vehicles with the exception of a three-tonner, which he loaded with Diesel oil and drove back to El Adem. For the next three days Major Rea, alone with his driver, tried to find his convoy although the area was overrun with enemy armoured formations.

And here is the story of Captain Francis Levens Cole, Durham Light Infantry, who on May 30 did great work with two sections of carriers. He attacked an enemy convoy, captured a lorry complete with crew, completely destroyed two more and shot up two lorry loads of infantry. The next day, with one section of carriers, four anti-tank guns and a section of machine-guns, Captain Cole set out to drive off 17 armoured vehicles which were protecting the same enemy convoy. In the face of heavy fire he had to withdraw, but not before he had been severely wounded and his driver killed. He was unable to get the driver out of his seat, so he held the dead man's leg on the accelerator and steered the carrier until he reached help.

On May 27, Second Lieutenant Robert Place, Durham Light Infantry, was in command of an outpost of his battalion when it was attacked in the early morning by a force estimated at an infantry battalion, supported by artillery. He fought at his post throughout the day and so controlled his arms that repeated attacks were driven off. Both of these officers received the Military Cross.

3.

THE break-through of the 50th Division form its position in the Gazala line—a remarkable feat of arms which will always be remembered — was, as I have pointed out. preceded by a great deal of confused fighting, in which units had done well. Of this period, officers and men have told me many curious stories.

There was, for instance, the case of an enemy tank which was chased and fired upon by three of our Bren carriers. Although bullets were harmlessly bouncing off its sides, the tank stopped and its Italian crew surrendered. Next day a D.L.I. platoon commander got permission to bring in the tank and later when some British sentries, not knowing what had happened, saw an enemy tank coming towards them, halting about 500 yards away, they got a shock. The episode caused some inter-unit rivalry and later on another group with three Bren carriers were delighted to find a second enemy tank, which they duly peppered. The tank stopped, but this time out popped an Italian head. "No make me prisoner," said a voice, "me on patrol." The Italian knew very well that Bren guns could not harm his tank and he hadn't enough heart to attack the carriers. All he wanted was to be allowed to patrol in peace !

After the enemy had had considerable success at Knightsbridge and were rapidly approaching and isolating Tobruk, it was decided that the 50th Division should break out in two groups through the Italian defensive ring in the west, push south beyond Bir Hacheim and then east towards the Egyptian frontier wire. Stores, equipment, mines and explosives which could not be carried were concentrated in dumps for demolition and destroyed on June 14.

Fortunately, owing to a sandstorm, the enemy was unable to observe, either from the ground or from the air, that transport was being brought up and portable stores loaded.

To avoid confusion I will outline the movements of No. 1 Group first. At eight that evening, a battalion of the East Yorks with artillery in support attacked the Italians in two waves. Two companies were held up for a time, but when they were joined by a third they broke down the enemy's resistance. Casualties were slight.

Singing "Rule Britannia," one platoon advanced in step towards the astonished Italians and it was not until they were within ten yards of the enemy that they adopted the 'on guard' position. Then, with bayonet, tommy gun, pistol and grenade, they put paid to any dugout showing signs of life.

This battalion of East Yorks successfully formed a bridgehead round the gap they had forced and a

URGENT
REPAIR

'THUMBS UP!'
ALWAYS

battalion of Green Howards, followed by Brigade Headquarters and an Ordnance company, passed through in the growing dusk which had become illuminated by the flames of burning vehicles and streaks of tracer. Shells were falling all around the vehicles, but actually slit trenches and dugouts took a far greater toll of these than the ill-judged fire of the Italians who had been surprised by the attack. Although some of our columns became split up and lost their direction, while others ran into a minefield, this group fared well on the whole and passed through several enemy leaguers or protected encampments unmolested, and finally reached the frontier wire after travelling sufficiently south to avoid Bir Hacheim.

A support company of Green Howards with an attachment of South African artillery was not so fortunate, for on arrival at a point known as Patrol Gap they found they could not go on owing to heavy shell fire. Accordingly, they waited until dawn and began withdrawing along the coast road towards Tobruk.

And now we will follow the fortunes of No. 2 Group, which also had to force a passage through the enemy's lines. This group consisted of 8th Durham Light Infantry (which with the attached troops made the bridgehead as the East Yorks had done in the case of Group No. 1), two other D.L.I. battalions, together with a carrier platoon of Green Howards, a section of machine-gunners and some South African armoured cars.

The 8th D.L.I. battalion left about nine o'clock on the evening of June 14 in three columns, B, C, and D, leaving its defended box with D column, which had a troop of guns and four armoured cars to the west ; C column to the east, with armoured cars and guns ; while in the middle was B column, consisting of the Commanding Officer and the majority of the men of the battalion, together with guns and machine-gunners from a Cheshire regiment, included in the 50th Division.

The western column had only advanced a mile when it met with stiff opposition from heavy machine-gun, anti-tank, mortar and small arms fire. The vehicle of the column commander was blown from under him, but the column managed to seize its objective and held on to it for four hours, after which it mopped up a German position some miles to the south.

The main column reached its objective without much opposition, although it lost about 50 men, including two officers.

A Lieutenant-Colonel, who was then a Major, described the experiences of C column, which he commanded. He said the column collected inside Stanley Gap in the brigade box and left late in the evening on a compass bearing for Patrol Grove, a flat-topped ridge. The enemy's attention was directed upon the blazing vehicles in the box, but his fire mostly passed over the heads of the men in the column which proceeded practically unharmed.

"We passed through two Italian positions before halting," he continued. "Not a soul could be seen though there were Italian arms and anti-tank guns everywhere which had been left loaded on the para-pets. Although it was believed that many Italians were lying at the bottom of their trenches, they were not disturbed.

"After forming a close leaguer on Patrol Grove ridge, the column sent out fighting and listening patrols. They discovered an Italian company posi-tion about 100 yards in front , while still another position was found level with us on the top of Patrol Grove. Here, about 100 Italians were seen forming up and being marched off south. This action did not seem to be approved by some of the men and much grumbling was heard.

"The fighting patrol entered an enemy batta-lion's signal exchange and an officers' mess. The value of silence was stressed and no one was allowed to fire a shot unless the leaguer was attacked. In fact, C column did not open fire during the night. Firing had been fairly heavy on the west side of Patrol Grove throughout the evening, but efforts to locate enemy machine-gun posts (to assist D column) were fruitless.

"About midnight the enemy position on top of Patrol Grove suddenly came to life. The position was defilated, but only 200 yards from our leaguer Italians could be seen lighting flares. One of our armoured cars inquisitively approached the lighted post and was hit and set on fire by anti-tank guns. During the next two hours several anti-tank guns and mortars continued to fire at it from the east side of the ridge.

"At two o'clock in the morning the column moved off along numerous tracks leading to Rotunda Mteifel and continually we had to tow vehicles out of abandoned slit-trenches and enemy positions. We were now moving in single file in the darkness and skirted several stationary enemy columns. Hereabouts, too, we struck a minefield and our rear vehicles, which contained some fitters, together with rations and extra water tanks, were blown up. Nothing was known about this at the head of the column until dawn when a party of 37 men under R.Q.M.S. Lightfoot caught up with us. They had walked seven miles, and the fact that they could overtake us shows how slow had been our progress through difficult country. At dawn it was also found that two platoons, two anti-tank guns and one 25-pounder were missing but actually this force reached the frontier safely before the rest of the column. The main body arrived at Fort Maddelena on the morning of June 16 and joined the other group."

There were, it will be recalled, two other battalions of Durham Light Infantry concerned in the
break-through. One encountered two minefields earlier on in which the navigator of the battalion was
wounded and his driver killed when a truck was
blown up. Under heavy fire a section of Sappers
made gaps through both minefields and the column,
passing through machine-gun and anti-tank fire with
few losses, completed the journey to the frontier.

Less one company which continued to hold
outpost positions, the 6th Durham Light Infantry
and attached troops had followed the 8th D.L.I.
and were themselves followed by Brigade Headquarters Group. The 9th D.L.I. with attached
artillery and engineers had been holding a defended
position to the east of 69 Brigade and was given the
option of following the rest of the Brigade or moving
independently via Tobruk. This Battalion Group
attempted to follow the remainder of the Brigade
but, on reaching the neighbourhood of the outposts
the Commander decided that, owing to burning
vehicles and the amount of firing taking place, that
line was inadvisable. He therefore turned about
and moved via the coast road and Tobruk.

Shortly after two in the morning, one company
of D.L.I. reached El Agheila Pass just before South
African troops cratered the road, but as it was passing through the defile it was heavily bombed by
low-flying aircraft and two 25-pounders were hit.
At El Mrassas, the head of the column came under
fire and some vehicles were set ablaze. The situa-

tion had to be cleared up quickly and it was decided
to attack the enemy's position on the escarpment.
South African armoured car patrols reported the
presence of six Mark III tanks and about a company
of infantry astride our line. The armoured cars,
together with Bren carriers and infantry, formed up
and attacked, practically wiping out all the enemy,
with little or no loss to our side. A 25-pounder was
being used against us over open sights, but a gunner
brought up his 2-pounder and did splendid work by
hitting the quad of the field gun, setting it ablaze.
Subsequently the enemy crew gave themselves up.

Later on, six enemy tanks launched an attack
and caused much damage to the rear of the column.
They were turning north and pursuing our armoured
cars when the same 2-pounder came into action
and, firing from a flank, set at least three of the tanks
ablaze, while our 25-pounders put others out of
action. During this engagement many of our infantry were forced into the sea and walked in water
to avoid enemy fire.

A curious incident occurred about this time.
An armoured car patrol noticed the unusual occurrence of a number of Arab women standing outside
their huts, and on investigation discovered that
30 German infantrymen were hiding inside. A burst
of Bren gun fire brought them out.

Divisional Signals had a rough passage with one
of the columns. During heavy shelling the driver
of the Officer Commanding was knocked out, being
hit on the jaw by a splinter. Verey lights went up

all round and a hail of inaccurate fire appeared to come from all directions, giving the impression that the car had stopped in the middle of an enemy leaguer owing to the height at which the incendiary bullets appeared to have been fired. After a short delay the car was restarted and driven at high speed, still followed by the amazing firework display.

The officer commanding Divisional Signals told me of a remarkable example of resource and initiative by the crew of a vehicle during the break-through. So near did the Signals' vehicle get to another enemy leaguer that Italian voices could be heard. Then the vehicle refused to budge, but rather than abandon it the crew decided to try repairs. It took them some time to discover that the fault was a burnt-out brush in the dynamo. There was no spare brush but they remembered that there were similar brushes in the generator of their wireless set. Accordingly, they removed one of the brushes and spent an hour shaping it to fit into the dynamo. Altogether the breakdown held them up for two hours and as soon as they moved off again machine-guns opened up on them.

On May 27 and 28, Rear Divisional Headquarters and the second line transport were threatened and attacked. Major Robert Turton, M.P. for Thirsk, who was Operational Staff Officer as well as D.A.A.G., was largely responsible for the safe withdrawal of the divisional lifeline and also showed conspicuous gallantry in face of enemy fire. He received the M.C.

Between May 27 and July 2, Lt. Col. Sydney Divers, O.B.E., commanding the R.A.S.C. and Rear

H.Q. of the 50th Division, kept the Division supplied and delivered troop-carrying transport in spite of enemy columns which frequently barred the way. Later, when Rear H.Q. and second line troops were attacked by armoured columns, Lt. Col. Divers quickly sized up the situation and disposed his small quota of fighting men with great skill, successfully withdrawing his columns. He was awarded the D.S.O.

Here's rather an old story about events which took place on June 14. Major Paul Parbury, who has received the M.C., was in command of a battery of field artillery operating with a battalion of the East Yorks. Just before dark, an East Yorks subaltern, thinking that the Major's carrier was one of the battalion's, ordered Major Parbury to "damned well" go and silence a machine-gun which was holding up his platoon's advance. Without hesitation the Major charged the post in his carrier. Having silenced the gun he returned to the subaltern and said : "I've done that." The subaltern still did not recognise him and told him to "damned well" silence another post and again Major Parbury, in spite of artillery and machine-gun fire, charged the post and silenced the gun.

Possibly it is not realised, except in the field, that anti-aircraft men are constantly operating with the infantry. On the night of June 14, Sergeant Georage Chapman Rae, Light A.A. Regiment, was in a column which was under heavy fire at less than a hundred yards range. His troop commander was wounded, his own tractor hit in the engine, the tractor immediately behind was on fire with ammunition exploding from it and several other nearby vehicles were burning and giving off a brilliant glare. In spite of all this, Sergeant Rae, who was awarded the M.M., found an abandoned vehicle and not only transferred his gun but all essential war stores from his tractor. He then drove away, carrying with him a number of wounded.

That same evening, Private Albert Robinson's company of East Yorks took part in an attack on a strongly held position, the object being to cover the closing of a gap in a minefield. There was very little cover and throughout the action the attack was subjected to heavy artillery, Breda and motorised machine-gun fire. On his own initiative, Robinson crawled 200 yards in front of his platoon headquarters between two enemy machine-gun posts, neither of which could fire without hitting the other. Settling himself comfortably, he proceeded to pick off the crews of the posts with great deliberation. Private Robinson was awarded the M.M.

Company Sergeant-Major Thomas Mattock, also of the East Yorks, went out accompanied by a Private and attacked and destroyed the whole crew of an enemy machine-gun post which had been holding up his company's advance. C.S.M. Mattock received the D.C.M.

And so one could go on giving example after example of courage and resource during these few days, but space will not permit.

4.

Two weeks after the Gazala episode, the enemy was surprised once more by "Fifty Div." and a gap was made in his positions in the Mersa Matruh area. The break-through here was inspired by the brilliant leadership of General Ramsden and was carried out at night through defiles offering an almost insuperable obstacle to the passage of vehicles.

During the night of June 16 the Division had collected in the Bir Thalata area. On June 21, a column formed mainly from 69 Brigade and all the divisional artillery took up positions about Buq Buq and, after the withdrawal of 10th Indian Division from Sollum on June 23, fought a rearguard action back to Matruh next day.

On June 25, the Division which, by this time, was very weak, was assembled and positioned on the escarpment south-east of Matruh. When the enemy crossed Siwa Road and passed south of Matruh on June 26/27 a good deal of fighting took place in this area.

On the night before the break-through a move was made into positions in wadis to the south-east of Gerawla. Ordered to attack the enemy's lines of communication and supported by light tanks it formed up into a number of columns. On the right in the Matruh Box itself, was the Indian Division (then commanded by a Major-General who, as Brigadier, had previously commanded a Brigade of the 50th); to the south were New Zealanders. As darkness fell, the columns of "Fifty Div." moved south over a wide front beating up any infantry it encountered with its 25 pounders and anti-tank guns. Presently, a mixed German and Italian force opened up with heavy fire, to which the columns replied vigorously, taking some prisoners. News then came through that the coast road to the east had been cut by the enemy. General Ramsden sat down beside his car and, in a noisy setting of shellfire and bombing, calmly made out orders for the Division to return immediately to clear the road. As a lover of aggressive action, he was pleased with the idea of chasing the enemy into the sea. And so, in the moonlight, back went the columns, the men welcoming the prospect of a fight and well satisfied with what they had accomplished during the day.

But, in point of fact, no fighting developed along the coast road, so the Division was ordered not only to repeat its performance of attacking lines of communication but to keep going and, eventually, take up a position on the other side of Fuka. That was if the enemy did not attack that evening, but if he did, orders were that the columns should stand and fight.

From the beginning things looked lively. A heavy enemy bombardment had put Mersa Matruh under a pall of smoke and dust ; our own guns were going all out as well and it seemed as though a big show was coming off. This was at about six o'clock in the evening.

Enemy gunners had got Divisional Headquarters well taped, for shells were falling uncomfortably close, though only one vehicle was destroyed. About 20 feet overhead, shell bursts made black blocks in the sky, while the ground was churned up by a hail of shells from a 105 mm. field gun. Small enemy guns then appeared on the hillside and fired over open sights, while tanks and parties of infantry were moving about menacingly until our artillery got on to them and reduced their activity. The situation did not look any too good for the safety of Headquarters and while General Ramsden was strolling quietly talking to the troops, staff officers, together with clerks, cooks, batmen and others, grabbed rifles and bandoliers and clambered up the sides of a wadi.

After a while it seemed that in spite of the considerable gunfire, the enemy's attack would not be on a full scale, so General Ramsden decided that the original orders for a break-through should be carried out.

Each of the several columns into which the Division was divided was given a different rendezvous, starting time and route out of the Mersa

Matruh area, and all the columns had to pass through steep, winding wadis, ascending to an escarpment in enemy hands. There were slit trenches as well as soft sand, both difficult enough for vehicles to negotiate at any time, but particularly so now since they could be overlooked by the enemy, and they had to move in single file to reach the top of the escarpment before it was light.

It was a grim undertaking and everybody knew that there would be familiar faces missing at the rendezvous next day. General Ramsden addressed his senior commanders and those in charge of the columns, wishing them good luck, while around the senior padre, Major Harlow, who is exceedingly popular in the Division, gathered a small circle of officers and men, to whom he gave his blessing.

It was now eight o'clock — just getting dark. Divisional Headquarters was being shelled; so was most of Mersa Matruh. The troops had been fighting all the previous night and had been shelled all day. They were extremely tired and rather dishevelled, and in the earlier encounters with the enemy against heavy odds they had lost most of their clothes, as well as valued personal possessions, such as photographs of their families, and letters. Yet, although prospects for the night seemed anything but rosy, they were full of confidence that the Division would pull off its dangerous task.

At dusk, the columns came up to their allotted area and one by one moved off in different directions, seeking their own way along the twisting wadis.

General Ramsden's own column, the adventures of which I will now describe, had just assembled when an enemy anti-tank gun which had been moved forward, opened fire. One truck was knocked out, but the other vehicles, including ambulances, moved forward as tracers flashed across the sky. So soft and deep was the sand in one wadi that a road had to be made, but General Ramsden solved the difficulty by uncovering the tarpaulins from the trucks, laying them over the sand and covering them with brushwood. In other wadis some vehicles became stuck, but a towing service was put into operation and at particularly bad patches trucks stood by to ex-, tricate those in difficulties. Time was precious for the columns were more or less in the enemy's lines and patrols were lurking nearby.

Shells were now falling on the high ground to which the wadis led. As it was taking a long time for the vehicles to pass the bad points, it seemed likely that the big traffic jams would be shelled.

Half way along one wadi a precipitous wall seemed insuperable. "I'm off," cried General Ramsden and throwing his coat to an officer tore about the wadi trying to find an alternative route. When he returned, dripping with sweat, he ordered a road to be made along a route he had decided upon. But the column was short of tarpaulins and when it was found that the wadi ended in a sheer 'face' or cul-de sac, the situation looked ominous. Climbing up

the side of the wadi, General Ramsden saw evidences
of a German patrol on the escarpment and sent out
a fighting patrol to deal with it. Meanwhile, at
three o'clock in the morning — only two hours to
go before the first light — vehicles were still trying
to climb prodigious slopes over small loose rocks.
Parties posted on either side of a chosen path were
organised for each vehicle. There was an anxious
pause when the first truck, an unloaded Morris 15,
made a dash for it, all its crew pushing behind. It
went up like a bird.

But how would the 3-ton lorries fare? That
was the question. Well, their difficulty was solved
by the square-nosed bantam runabouts, known as
Jeeps. These splendid American-built vehicles are
admirably suited for the desert for they defy soft
sand. (They have a four-wheel drive and their
engines develop 60 h.p.). The Jeeps pushed up the
lorries with men behind shoving for all they were
worth.

At last all the vehicles managed to scramble up
somehow and, after assembling on top, dashed south-
wards, chasing every German and Italian vehicle
in sight. One German armoured car got the shock
of its life when it found itself being pursued by a
15-cwt. truck.

For 30 miles the columns pushed on, then turned
east. By this time many vehicles were being towed,
while others had to be destroyed as useless. Just

how fast 3-tonners can travel was proved when they outpaced the General's battle car and evaded tanks which were chasing them.

General Ramsden's vehicle, a staff car with its hood cut off, proved to be one of the most difficult to get up the sides of the wadi. It could only go up steep hills in reverse and when it was ascending one incline thus, its fender became stuck in that of the Jeep which was pushing it. The Jeep had to be lifted up by a party of men before the General's car could be extricated.

Fuka, the original rendezvous for the Division, was found to be in German hands, so the columns went on to the El-Alamein — Ruweisat line to take part in stemming Rommel's advance to the Nile Delta. One brigade was engaged in heavy fighting here. (This occurred too recently to be described in this narrative.)

Meanwhile, the Indian Division occupying Matruh and the plateau to the east and south of the town, who had done extremely well in fierce fighting, made a remarkable getaway.

In the Charing Cross section, which lay in the path of the enemy, who was advancing along the road from El Adem in his sweep forward, a brigade was hotly engaged all day and all the following night. Another brigade, finding its way to the east completely barred, broke through to the south, on the flank of the 50th Division.

One evening, an enemy column, consisting of no fewer than 100 tanks and 3,000 transports, passed right along the route the Brigade was taking. The Brigadier brought out his brigade with very few losses, having carried out a very clever move south-wards, which consisted of making a number of abrupt turns to the west, and then back again.

Though short of artillery and anti-tank guns, 50 Div. completed its break-through. Previously, some units had come in for very rough handling in the positions they occupied south of Garawla, about 14 miles from Matruh, and there were many awk-ward situations due to lack of information in a confused situation, in which it was most difficult to establish the exact position of the enemy.

In the case of one battalion, the units were so overrun that only Headquarters company and the remnants of the Support company could continue fighting. They knocked out several enemy tanks before they were ordered to withdraw. One cap-tured party consisting of five or six officers, a ser-geant-major and 200 men, sent off in its own vehicles under escort, somehow managed to head northwards until it ran into Indian defended localities, and it was the escort and not the party that ended up as prisoners.

Sergeant-Major Armstrong told me that before they were captured the Germans came at them with the bayonet, followed by a cover of infantry with

Spandau guns. Armstrong said he did not mind so much surrendering his binoculars, but he was extremely reluctant to hand over his regimental presentation watch. He did so, however, at the point of the bayonet. The Sergeant-Major was impressed by the efficiency of German methods. He observed that the first wave of an infantry attack is made up of troops with bayonets, the second by men armed with light automatics and the third by salvage squads, whose job it is to collect prisoners. First of all they hand over the prisoners to the field ambulance units who require them to bring in any wounded. Prisoners of war then find that all their kit has been neatly packed into bundles, according to its category, and the men can collect clothing as well as food and water before marching off. A series of photographs is taken of prisoners and their belongings at the field ambulance

Like every British soldier to whom I have spoken, Armstrong has a high opinion of the work of the R.A.F. and remarked that the *Luftwaffe* does not give anything like such a big safety margin as we do when machine-gunning is carried out from the air.

Countless noble deeds were done by isolated packets of encircled men of the 50th Division, who fought on until their last round of ammunition was expended ; and there were many break-throughs to safety by officers and men who wandered for three or four days with very little food and water in order to gain our lines at El Alamein, some trudging southwards and going through part of the Qattara depression. During the fighting there were many cases where troops, who had been overrun, succeeded in knocking out many enemy tanks and transport vehicles.

The award of the Military Cross to a Warrant Officer is a rare honour, but it fell to R.S.M. Arthur Page, Durham Light Infantry, who, on June 27, was in charge of a platoon of a company ordered to hold the escarpment at Bir Hamam as an outpost. The position was attacked and although commanding only a mixed platoon, which included clerks, R.S.M. Page put such heart into the men that the rear sections held on doggedly after the forward section had been captured.

With armoured cars within150 yards range, R.S.M. Page repeatedly stood up and sniped at the commanders as they tried to open their turrets. Later, working round to the right, he brought an abandoned 2-pounder into action and personally knocked out a self-propelling gun ; he also put the enemy commander's car out of action and killed the officer

R.S.M. Page was wounded in the leg at the beginning of the action but nobody knew about it until the operation was over.

Lieutenant-Colonel Thomas Stansfield, Green Howards, was awarded the D.S.O. for commanding a battalion of the East Yorks. whose success in forming a bridgehead in the Matruh area was to a large extent due to him.

Lieutenant-Colonel Edward Cooke-Collis, Green Howards, who had distinguished himself in action in earlier operations, was wounded near Mersa Matruh while in command of the 69th Brigade. Refusing to be evacuated, he remained in action commanding his brigade with his wounded arm in a sling. On June 28, when the brigade, with the rest of the Division, was surrounded, the Colonel (who has received the D.S.O.) conducted its breakthrough the enemy lines will skill and conspicuous bravery. Perhaps it is fitting here to mention the fact that Lt. Col. M.L.P. Jackson, Green Howards, commanding a battalion of Durham Light Infantry, and Lt. Col. Jocelyn E.S. Percy, M.C., Durham Light Infantry, were also among the senior officers of the Division who received the D.S.O. for magnificent achievements during the period May 27 to June 14.

DESERT
HALT

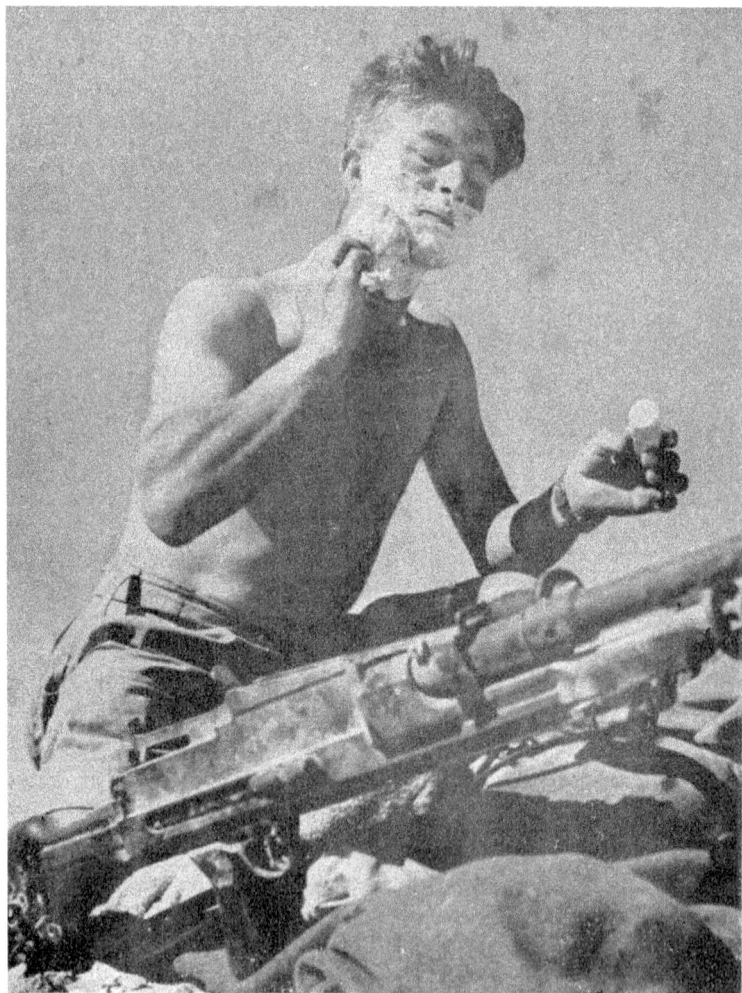

MORNING

5

IT must be very difficult for the non-military reader to realise the immensity of a division or to understand its machinery. I imagine that were all the vehicles to be spread out in a column along a road with the proper distance between them, the space occupied would not fall far short of 200 miles.

When divisions carry out manoeuvres in England, acute difficulties arise regarding space, but in the vast open areas of the desert where there are practically no houses and certainly no crops, not only can the largest formations function as a whole, but they can actually be swallowed up; that is why there are so many surprises, and at times our own and enemy columns apparently appear from nowhere.

There is another point which perhaps is not appreciated. Much is said and written about co-operation between land and air forces, but little or nothing about the cooperation required between men of widely different trades and traditions. When you have infantry, field artillery, machine-gunners, R.A.S.C. and Ordnance personnel combined with sappers, signallers, military police and other elements as a body, there will be something like chaos in action (or on the move) unless there exists a general sentiment of loyalty and affection for the Division as a whole, as well as complete confidence in its leader.

Some wise observations were made to me by the officer commanding the R.A.S.C. Territorial unit, which serves the 50th Division. This unit was originally based upon Hull, but contains a large number of men from the North Country generally. Some of its officers once sat at adjoining desks at school with N.C.O's and Privates now under their command. This close association may account in some measure for the unity of outlook just as geographical factors help to maintain the *esprit de corps* in the Division.

"The individual driver is a very important person," said the Colonel, "and it seems to me that however efficient may be the chain of the Army's organisation from the War Office in London to G.H.Q., Middle East, right down to the units in the line, a big issue may actually be decided by an individual driver carrying on with his job in a 3-tonner, and very often alone. I often point this out to the boys and there is always a response. When you are writing about the Division, emphasise the spirit of inter-help which is so much in evidence.

"The infantryman has complete faith in the R.A.S.C. and the R.A.S.C. has complete faith in him. A similar remark would apply to the relationships between the other services. There is an astonishingly keen team spirit and I've never known of a case in which a skilled soldier in his own line has said to another equally skilled in his, 'This is really your job, you know.'

"Drivers are ready to pick up their rifles at any mement and defend a position, while infantrymen who can drive are ready to take their places when the drivers are tired. And, incidentally, our drivers sometimes get no sleep for 48 hours on end. This spirit of cooperation has been fostered by General Martel, who once commanded the Division, and by General Ramsden, as well as by the present Commander.

"There's a fighting spirit alongside it. We've only one task and that is to hit the enemy, hit him hard and go on hitting him. That's the sentiment existing as much among the men working in the cookhouses as among the more defined fighting troops. Were the Boche to poke his nose into a divisional cookhouse at this moment, he would certainly get a butcher's knife stuck into him as well as being peppered by bully beef tins as a preliminary to further action."

I am told there is a corporal from Hull in the Division who lost his father and mother, and his wife and three children, in an air raid. He has only one child left but he has never made a request to return to England. All he wants is to get at the enemy.

Of the Division's aggressive spirit I heard an amusing instance the other day. During a confused struggle over a wide area, some Yorkshiremen were found manning a slit trench miles from anywhere.

"What are you doing?" asked a New Zealand Colonel.

"Oh, just mooking oop Jerry," was the reply.

Which reminds me, *à propos*, of a little yarn told me by a friend who was bathing in Tobruk during the siege. Stukas came down and dive-bombed the beach and he thought it advisable to swim out to sea. There seemed to be no one else about but, presently, out of the water popped a head with a placid face.

"Where on earth have you come from?" said my friend.

"Newcrstle, sir," replied the man, and without another word he waded ashore and dressed himself.

In the Gazala line, besides living with battalions on column work, the R.A.S.C. maintained the Division's lifeline and operated on supply convoys, involving a turn round of 180 miles. The men would be on the road for as many as 26 to 30 hours at a time.

When the enemy came round to the east of our line, supplies for the Division had first to come westwards along the coast road from Tobruk, then up the escarpment at Gazala (where drivers were frequently dive-bombed) and, finally, across no-man's-land to the divisional boxes. To reach the position of one brigade, lorries had to go through enemy country to the rear of Bir Hacheim. During one period, playing a game of hide and seek with the enemy, drivers spent three days trying to find an entrance and relied upon their wits, speed, observation and skill to avoid capture or destruction of their vehicles.

As they were in the path of the enemy's advance, R.A.S.C. vehicles had to cut across columns of tanks and armoured cars and run the gauntlet of machine-gun fire. The enemy became confused by this performance and at times were so surprised to see a mass of transport approaching that they sheered off. Occasionally the drivers succeeded in taking some prisoners. On the whole, the vehicles managed to smash their way through with little loss. Supplies must get there : that was the drivers' determination and there was seldom a day during the most difficult period when the fighting troops failed to get all they needed ; rarely was there a shortage of water, rations or even N.A.A.F.I. stores.

Due to General Ramsden's foresight, the Division found that the R.A.S.C. had arrived four hours before they arrived at the frontier after the break-through, enabling the formations to function perfectly and be ready for immediate action.

Here are the stories of two gallant actions for which Captain Harold Butterworth and Lieutenant Horace Jenkins were awarded the Military Cross.

On May 28, Captain Butterworth was ordered to take a convoy of lorries to collect ammunition from Tobruk, although it was not known whether the road had been reached by a large enemy force operating in the area. Travelling half a mile ahead of his convoy, which he moved by a series of bounds, Captain Butterworth sighted enemy fighting vehicles. Drivers of other convoys which had turned back told him that the enemy had cut the road, but he decided to risk it. Captain Butterworth reached Tobruk, loaded up with ammunition, but was then refused permission to leave as the enemy was astride the road. Finally he was told he could go at his own risk. He travelled a short distance in the night and pushed ahead in broad daylight. Although the road was under direct fire at one point as well as being dive-bombed, Captain Butterworth, by skilful handling, got his convoy through without losing a single vehicle.

On May 27, Lt. Jenkins was in command of nine ammunition lorries destined for 150 Brigade box. Prevented by shell-fire from taking the normal route, he found an alternative way and delivered seven of his loads. An hour passed and the other two lorries were still missing. In spite of heavy shelling he went back and found that the vehicles had been destroyed, but he rescued the drivers and returned to the box. He then took his convoy back through country overrun by the enemy. Finding his original refilling point in enemy hands he went to Tobruk. Twice his convoy was bombed and machine-gunned, but he finally reported on May 29 with ten loads of ammunition, having added three lost vehicles to his convoy.

6.

ESCAPES from death that seem almost miraculous are not of infrequent occurrence in the desert. There was one case I remember of a shell bursting right in front of one man. A cloud of yellow smoke and dust hid him from view and nobody expected to see any vestige of him again. He emerged, however, without showing any signs of being shaken by the experience, though was ruefully examining one finger and complained of sprain.

The other day I talked to Private A. Baines, of Dewsbury, who, regarding me solemnly through steel-rimmed spectacles, told me of another escape for which I can find no reasonable explanation. Baines, who has a round placid face, is batman to a major at the headquarters of the 50th Division. After the break-through from the Mersa Matruh area the major, who was with a sergeant in an anti-tank rifle pit, instructed Baines to take a message to the General. Baines had only got five yards from the pit when a shell burst a foot in front of him. The sergeant in the pit was wounded but Baines was untouched. "I felt the blast a bit," he said "and it certainly shook me up." Baines delivered his message although shells were dropping every ten yards or so along his path.

Some distance away, I met Sergeant R. Martin, a fellow journalist, who is one of those enviable people who not only begins a diary but continues writing it up it is finished. He has been writing diaries for months, but of course they are all tucked away at the base, for one does not carry diaries about here ; in fact, directly I have sent any despatch, I discard all copies and notes. It will be a relief to find later that in the period of garrulous senility I shall have reached by the time this war is over, I cannot complete in the war book market which will be swamped by people with inside stories. My material will be missing and happily forgotten.

Sergeant Martin had, however, his most recent volume with him and, fishing it out of a locker, gave me this story about the Divisional Field Ambulance, the background for which is the confused fighting round Acroma. The Field Ambulance was captured seven times : one main dressing station was never seen again and another was overrun for three days.

"Some Germans removed our staff cars and carried them off," said Sergeant Martin. "We had all been wondering why they had not taken our Commanding Officer with them and when in the evening a large staff car swept in (we had got used to these lightning visits by the Jerries by that time) and a lieutenant emerged and asked to speak to the

C.O., we thought the time had come for saying good-bye to him. To our surprise, however, this six-foot tall officer, speaking perfect English, gave the most punctilious salute, 'I've come to apologise for some of my men taking personal kit this morning and I've brought it back'. We thought there must be a catch, but he went on : 'We have orders not to take kit or interfere with medical units if avoidable' and, reaching into his car with the showmanlike gesture of a conjuror producing rabbits out of a hat, he held up a kit-bag. We thought this was a suitable moment to ask for the return of our radios. You shall have them back,' said Jerry, but just then came the whine and screech of a shell, which burst a short distance away. We dived into slit trenches and I had the greatest pleasure in the world when I found I had alighted right on the neck of a Jerry N.C.O. and I rammed his face in the bottom of the trench. He eventually scrambled out and ran for the car with his officer. We never saw them again, but I heard the lieutenant call out : 'Those radios, they'll be returned... on a more suitable occasion !''

The Divisional Field Ambulance has done well in the matter of decorations. I will give just one example of courage from an impressive list.

Sergeant Walter Doxford was in a column which was being heavily bombed. As soon as the raid was over, he got out his section equipment, opened up a dressing station and carried on with his duties as senior N.C.O. until he collapsed. Only then was it discovered by his officer that he had a severe wound in the chest, penetrating to the lung. He was awarded the M.M.

To deal adequately with the activities of the batteries of the Royal Artillery cooperating with other arms during the long series of engagements, which I have attempted to describe in outline, would demand a whole series of articles. I cannot attempt the task now, but possibly just one account of gallantry will convey some idea of the behaviour of the divisional gunners in action.

On June 15, Captain John Irvine's armoured observation post was blown up by a mine and he became separated from his troops. He obtained another truck and on his way to rejoin his guns found a second troop engaging some tanks. Together with the troop commander and a warrant officer, he manned one gun until it was knocked out. After seeing to the evacuation of the commander, who was wounded, Captain Irvine took charge and for five hours under continual shellfire reorganised the depleted detachments, saw that enough vehicles were made serviceable to withdraw the guns, and supervised the evacuation of the wounded. After withdrawing some guns to safety across a wadi under very heavy shellfire, he recrossed the wadi twice to arrange the removal of other vehicles. He took away the sights from one gun as the tractor containing ammunition was burning a few yards away... Captain Irvine received the M.C.

I had a talk with the Officer Commanding Divisional Signals, who are justifiably proud of the fact that ten of their original officers have attained the rank of Lieutenant-Colonel. The O.C. discussed the technical difficulties of keeping communications going in duststorms, and of electrical disturbances which cause sparking in wireless sets.

In the desert, men of the Royal Corps of Signals have stood by their sets for 24 hours at a stretch, while linesmen have had a terrific job doing repairs, as tanks and other vehicles constantly cut across telephone wires stretched for miles along the ground.

The Colonel told me of one field telephone exchange operator who is an exceedingly polite man. He knows all the conciliatory phrases and all the answers. One day, bullets were puncturing holes in his vehicle as he sat plugging in calls. The hotter things got the more polite he became. "Sorry, but the line has been blown up," he would explain, or, "If you would kindly hold the line I'll endeavour to connect you, but at the moment..."

I was glad to hear the Colonel pay a tribute to the fortitude of wounded men of the Division. After there had been a direct hit on a truck," he said, "I travelled from Matruh on various conveyances in the company of seriously wounded men. We were so crowded that there wasn't room to move and no proper medical attention could be given. Yet far from grousing, everyone had a smile and most of the men cracked jokes. It was a most impressive performance.''

The Colonel asked me to say how grateful are the men of the Division to the Northumberland and Durham War Needs Fund. The sum of £1,000 was received not long ago for distribution. The money went to buy sports gear, wireless sets and much needed books and magazines, of which there can never be too many.

I have left to the last one constituent unit which possibly ought to have been mentioned among the first, since the fighting troops are as much dependent upon Ordnance services as upon food and water. It is clear that since the R.A.S.C. is concerned with the maintenance of its own vehicles, as distinct from those of Ordnance, and yet takes up ordnance stores with the rations, first-class cooperation between the two services is essential, and this has certainly been reached in the Division. Within the Ordnance unit itself, cooperation is vital between men of at least 11 different skilled trades. Mechanical problems are immense in the desert. Keeping springs repaired is an essential part of the maintenance work, while sand and grit cause stoppages in the petrol flow and engines overheat in following winds, causing delays and using up valuable water.

With two officers, the A.D.O.S. keeps the Division supplied with everything mechanical, besides supervising vehicles' maintenance. The Ordnance service of the Division has never failed.

Strange though it may seem, I doubt whether any stories about recovery lorries under fire have been published, so it seems all the more attractive to mention this quite typical incident concerning two lorries, a Crossley and a six-wheeled Leyland, which came under machine-gun fire at night. Such vehicles are usually more important than these they recover, and in this case their height caused them to be silhouetted against the skyline and picked out as targets.

A shell from an anti-tank gun hit the Leyland, killed a man and blew up the reserve petrol tank, but the vehicles were able to proceed, together with a 15-cwt. Ford and a 3-ton Chevrolet. The column was subjected to intense machine-gun fire for over a mile. It avoided many enemy columns but actually followed one for some distance before it was realised the column was hostile. Later, the Ordnance officer in charge discovered to his surprise a useable staff car containing kit, and it dawned on him that Fuka aerodrome which he was approaching was in enemy hands. He then found that the car would not start and no sooner had he put it in tow than a recovery lorry became stuck in soft sand and the water impellor began to leak. Although three out of the four vehicles were hit, the El Alamein position was eventually reached. Not a very exciting story, you may say, but it serves the purpose of indicating that in desert warfare technicians face precisely similar perils as fighting troops, while their job — especially during and after battles when almost everything depends upon speed in recovery, getting damaged vehicles and guns away — is vitally important.

Just a paragraph or two about the Divisional Royal Engineers. It may be mentioned as a strange fact that Sappers get far less publicity, if that is the right word, than any other soldier, although their work is exacting and dangerous enough, especially in the desert, where there are countless miles of minefields.

At Gazala, Sappers of the 50th Division laid about 150,000 mines, besides working on water supplies. They sank many shafts for water and cleared *birs* or ancient cisterns for storing it, but unfortunately these were captured during the first few days of the enemy's offensive. In one area alone, 20 enemy tanks were disabled by our mines.

There was also much mine-lifting. On one occasion when a company found Italians laying French mines, it picked up 1,200 of these in the dark.

A Lance-Sergeant, accompanied by a Sapper, came across an officers' mess by chance in the German lines and heard a vigorous argument going on inside.

They were consequently unheard when they laid fixed charges on the corners of the dug-in tent. Having set the pencil, they retired to hear with gratification four explosions, and they were well out of range when machine-guns opened up on them.

Another party of Sappers, accompanied by men of the D.L.I., crept up to four large enemy tanks, the crews of which were inside. A Lance-Corporal put charges in all the tanks, sufficiently powerful to blow off the sprocket wheels. They also heard satisfactory bangs on the way home.

At Martuba, one company carried an observation post 20 feet high and although they could erect this in two minutes, a gunner officer was acutally on his way up before that.

It is no particular joke laying mines in the darkness, especially when there's a rocky surface ; but pulling them up is even more difficult and urduous.

* * *

Well, there is an outline — I cannot call it anything else — of the story of "Fifty Div." The full account, when it comes to be written, will be one of the most remarkable of this war. It is in circumstances of adversity and bad luck that the finest qualities of soldiers are displayed. This has been less of a record of triumphant success than of fortitude displayed under great difficulties and handicaps.

The War Correspondent is sometimes accused of being over — optimistic, and to such a charge I could plead guilty on many occasions : yet finding oneself among such men as these and hearing stories of much heroism and endurance, it has been difficult to take cold, detached views.

Up to the time these somewhat disjointed articles were written, things had not gone well. But when they were being reprinted for their present purpose the situation had so altered as to give grounds for reasonable confidence and we were more than ever certain that ultimately our optimism will be justified. Whatever lies ahead the performance of the 50th Division in the desert will — when the history of these most difficult times is recorded — form one of its most glorious chapters and it will be shown how it has added great lustre to British military traditions.

REGIMENTAL HISTORIES
OF THE BRITISH ARMY

A SELECTION OF N&MP REPRINTED TITLES
ALWAYS AVAILABLE ALWAYS IN PRINT

∽

READ THE REAL HISTORY OF THE SECOND WORLD WAR IN THE STORIES OF THE REGIMENTS, CORPS, DIVISIONS, & BATTALIONS THAT FOUGHT IT.

NAVAL & MILITARY
PRESS
WWW.NAVAL-MILITARY-PRESS.COM

CLUB ROUTE IN EUROPE
The Story of 30 Corps in
the European Campaign.
9781783311033

30 Corps was heavily involved in the closing
campaigns of the Second World War in Europe,
starting when its 50th (Northumbrian)
Division landed on Gold Beach on D-day. It
helped to clear the Cotentin peninsular in
Operation Bluecoat and, after General Brian
Horrocks took over command, it took part in
Operation Market Garden at Arnhem, and the
crossing of the Rhine into the German
heartland. A superb unit history of these often
difficult and bloody operations.

SEVENTH ARMOURED DIVISION
October 1938 - May 1943
9781474539180

2nd BATTALION SOUTH WALES BORDERS 24th REGIMENT
D-DAY TO VE-DAY
9781474539012

Describing the campaign from D-Day onwards, this excellent contemporary battalion
history is divided into two parts. The first contains an outline of the activities of the
2/24th during the campaign in Europe from D-Day to VE-Day, and the second is a
detailed narrative of some of the more important actions in which the battalion fought.
Complete with a list of awards. Originally printed in Hamburg in 1945.

49 (WEST RIDING) RECONNAISSANCE REGIMENT
Royal Armoured Corps - Summary of Operations June 1944 to May 1945
9781474536677

Rare Reconnaissance unit history that was completed immediately after the war had
ended. Following the D-Day invasions, the 49th Reconnaissance Regiment fought as
Montgomery's left flank, and played vital roles in the capture of Arnhem, and the
liberation of Holland. They are honoured annually in Utrecht to this day. The book is
completed with 2 good coloured maps.

THE HISTORY OF THE CORPS OF ROYAL MILITARY POLICE
9781783310951
Excellent history of this corps, almost entirely devoted to WW2 on all fronts, including
Middle East, North-West Europe and Burma. Complete with a Roll of Honour.

THE STORY OF THE 79th ARMOURED DIVISION OCTOBER 1942 - JUNE 1945
9781783310395

A magnificent and fully illustrated official history of Britain's 79th Armoured Division - the specialised unit which developed and operated 'Hobart's Funnies', the adapted tanks which carried out a range of tasks on D-day and after ranging from mine clearance to bridge laying. Follows the unit from its formation to victory in Europe.

HISTORY OF THE ARGYLL & SUTHERLAND HIGHLANDERS 7th BATTALION
From El Alamein To Germany
9781781519653

THE ESSEX REGIMENT 1929 - 1950
9781781519813

Comprehensive history of both regular & territorial force battalions, mainly Middle East (inc. Tobruk & Alamein), North-West Europe & 1st Bn. with Chindits in Burma 1944. Rolls of Honour and awards.

HISTORY OF THE IRISH GUARDS IN THE SECOND WORLD WAR
9781474537094

A fine history of a proud regiment; The Irish Guards played their part gallantly during campaigns in Europe, North Africa and Italy during the Second World War, claiming two Victoria Cross recipients during that conflict. The basis of this history was the War Diaries kept by Battalion Intelligence Officers, along with individual records and papers. A Roll of Honour, Honours Awards down to Military Medal, and 22 good maps complete this very good WW2 Regimental.

ALGIERS TO AUSTRIA
The 78th Division in the Second World War
9781783310265

OPERATIONS OF THE EIGHTH CORPS
The River Rhine to the Baltic Sea. A narrative account of the pursuit and final defeat of the German Armed Forces March-May 1945.
9781474538176

THE HISTORY OF THE 51st HIGHLAND DIVISION 1939-1945
9781474536660

The 51st Highland Division fought and lost in France in 1940, was reborn, and fought and won in the North African desert, Sicily and finally in North Western Europe from D-Day to the end of the war. As a division the men earned the respect of friend and foe alike, and this is their story. Amply illustrated with 36 photographs, 18 maps and battle plans (many coloured) that help the reader to follow the course of the conflict. A good index (persons, units and place names) and a statistical battle casualties list complete this good WW2 Divisional History

THE HISTORY OF THE FIFTEENTH SCOTTISH DIVISION 1939-1945
9781783310852

Formed at the outbreak of war in September 1939, the 15th (Scottish) division served in North-western Europe after landing in Normandy soon after D-day on 14 June 1944 . It fought on the Odon River, at Caen, Caumont, Mont Pincon, the Nederrijn, the Rhineland, and across the Rhine. On April 10, 1946, the division was disbanded. The total number of casualties it sustained during the 12 months of fighting was 11,772.

THE STORY OF THE ROYAL ARMY SERVICE CORPS, 1939-1945
9781474538251

A complete history of the RASC in all theatres throughout the Second World War. This a model unit history originally published under the direction of the Institution of the Royal Army Service Corps, it is excellently produced, and arranged by theatre of war. The narrative is full with technical information, and the many photographic plates record visually British military vehicles in service situations.